KU-189-224

The Wild Side of Pet
Fish

Jo Waters

www.raintreepublishers.co.uk

Visit our website to find out more information about **Raintree** books.

To order:

☎ Phone 44 (0) 1865 888112

🖹 Send a fax to 44 (0) 1865 314091

🖥 Visit the Raintree Bookshop at **www.raintreepublishers.co.uk** to browse our catalogue and order online.

First published in Great Britain by
Raintree, Halley Court, Jordan Hill, Oxford
OX2 8EJ, part of Harcourt Education.
Raintree is a registered trademark of Harcourt
Education Ltd.

© Harcourt Education Ltd 2004
The moral right of the proprietor has been
asserted.

Editorial: Melanie Copland and Saskia Besier
Design: Richard Parker and
Tinstar Design Ltd (www.tinstar.co.uk)
Picture Research: Maria Joannou and Alison Prior
Production: Duncan Gilbert

Originated by Ambassador Litho Ltd
Printed and bound in China by South China
Printing Company

The paper used to print this book comes from
sustainable resources.

ISBN 1 844 43478 8
08 07 06 05 04
10 9 8 7 6 5 4 3 2 1

**British Library Cataloguing in Publication
Data**
Waters, Jo
The Wild Side of Pet Fish
639.3
A full catalogue record for this book is available
from the British Library.

Acknowledgements
The publishers would like to thank the following
for permission to reproduce photographs: Bruce
Coleman Collection pp. **5 right**, **10** (Pacific
Stock), **8 top** (Hans Reinhard), **7** (Jane Burton);
Corbis pp. **24** (S Westmorland), **5 left**; Getty
Images p. **29** (Photodisc); Nature Picture Library
pp. **8 bot** (David Hall), **17** (Brandon Cole);
NHPA pp. **11** (T McDonald), **15** (G I Bernard),
28; Oxford Scientific Films p. **4** (D Fleetham), **12**
(Z Leszczynski), **16**, **19** (M Gibbs), **22** (K Tyrell),
26 (R Kuiter), **27** (M Deeble & V Stone), **23**;
Photographers Direct pp. **14** (Joe Bellantoni), **25**
(Krys Bailey); Tudor Photography/Harcourt
Education Ltd pp. **9**, **21**.

Cover photograph of Festival Platy fish,
reproduced with permission of Oxford Scientific
Films (Max Gibbs). Inset cover photograph of a
great white shark reproduced with permission of
Nature Picture Library (Brandon Cole).

The publishers would like to thank Michaela
Miller for her assistance in the preparation of this
book.

Every effort has been made to contact copyright
holders of any material reproduced in this book.
Any omissions will be rectified in subsequent
printings if notice is given to the publishers.

Contents

Was your pet once wild? 4

Types of fish 6

Saltwater and freshwater 8

Fish habitats. 10

Fish anatomy 12

How do fish breathe? 14

Senses 16

Movement 18

What do fish eat? 20

Do fish live in groups? 22

Sleeping 24

Life cycle of a fish 26

Common problems 28

Find out for yourself 30

Glossary. 31

Index 32

Any words appearing in bold, **like this**, are explained in the Glossary.

Was your pet once wild?

You may think that you just have a pet fish, but really you have a wild animal living in your home. Finding out about the wild side of your pet fish will help you to give it a better life.

There are many types of fish in the wild. They live all over the world in rivers, lakes and seas.

Sharks
Sharks are the biggest fish.

This fish hiding in **coral** is the world's smallest fish, the dwarf goby. The female hardly ever grows more than 1 centimetre long.

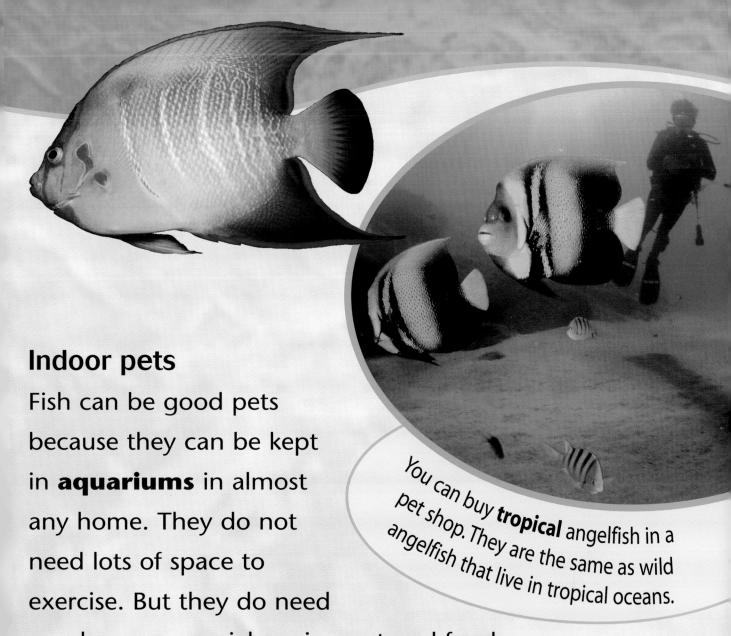

Indoor pets

Fish can be good pets because they can be kept in **aquariums** in almost any home. They do not need lots of space to exercise. But they do need regular care, special equipment and food.

You can buy **tropical** angelfish in a pet shop. They are the same as wild angelfish that live in tropical oceans.

There are many types of fish you can keep in aquariums. You can even keep some fish like koi carp in a pond in your garden.

Most pet fish are really wild ones that have been caught.

5

Types of fish

Fish live in **tropical** areas and also in the cooler parts of the world. Examples of tropical fish include angelfish, piranhas and cichlids. Coldwater fish include many of the types of fish we eat, such as salmon, trout and tuna.

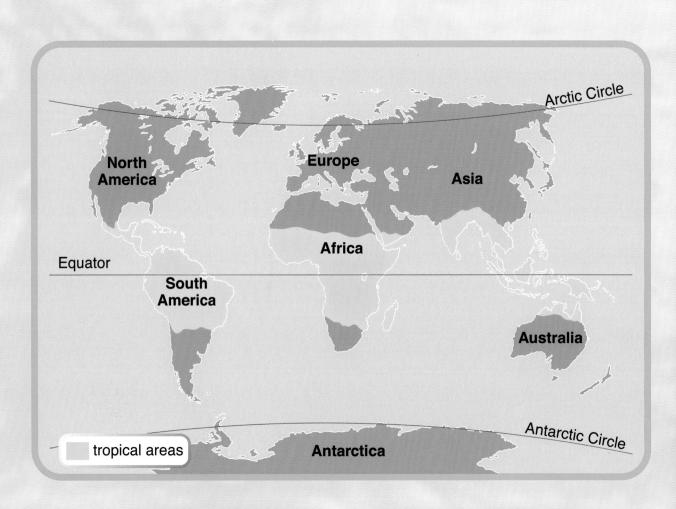

This map shows tropical areas of the world. These are warm places next to the **equator**, such as parts of South America and Africa.

Warm and cold

Many pet fish originally came from tropical areas. These fish need the water in their **aquarium** to be heated because the water in their natural **habitat** is warm. You can buy heating equipment at pet shops.

You can also keep coldwater fish as pets. Popular choices include goldfish, minnows, guppies, loaches or tench. You should never keep coldwater fish and tropical fish together as they need different temperatures and food.

Goldfish are the most popular pets today.

Pet goldfish
Goldfish are only meant to be pets and would not survive very well in the wild.

7

Saltwater and freshwater

Saltwater fish live in seas and oceans, where the water contains a lot of salt. Freshwater fish live in lakes and rivers, where the water is not salty.

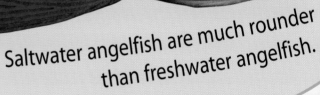

Saltwater angelfish are much rounder than freshwater angelfish.

Different looks

Freshwater fish often have large, delicate fins and very beautiful colours. Saltwater fish are usually stronger than freshwater fish. This is because they live in the sea and need to swim against strong **currents** and waves. They are more muscular and look rounder.

Most people keep freshwater fish, such as tetras and barbs.

Saltwater fish are very hard to look after. The water has to have exactly the right amount of salt. Only experts should keep saltwater fish.

Tank cleaning

The water in your **aquarium** needs to be kept fresh and clean. Dirty water is bad for your fish. Take a little water out of the tank and replace it with clean water every one to two weeks.

Scrape the glass of the aquarium every few weeks to get rid of any **algae**.

9

Fish habitats

Most fish need places to shelter from strong **currents**, to hide from **predators** and to sleep. For example, many fish live on **coral reefs**. Coral reefs are mostly found in **tropical** and warm oceans. Coral is actually an animal that grows on rocks.

The ray lives on the sandy bottom of the ocean and can bury itself in sand for **camouflage**.

The piranha lives in tropical rivers. Plants grow in tropical rivers, providing shelter and food for the fish.

These reef fish live amongst the coral.

Making a habitat

Plants make your fish's **aquarium** more like its wild **habitat**. Fish can eat the plants and hide in them. There are many suitable water-plants that you can buy. You can buy plastic plants as well. Make sure your tank is big enough for all your fish.

Gravel makes a good covering for the bottom of the tank. It helps to hold plants in place.

Fish anatomy

Most fish have the same basic **anatomy** or body parts. They have scales covering their bodies. Scales make the fish smooth in the water and protect it from injury. All fish have fins and **gills**. Fins keep the fish upright and are sometimes used to help the fish swim forwards or stop.

Eels are muscular, bony fish with long thin bodies. They look more like snakes than fish.

Electric eels can grow to over 2 metres long.

Electric fish!
*Electric eels are special because they can make **electricity** in their bodies. They can shock their **prey** or **predators**.*

12

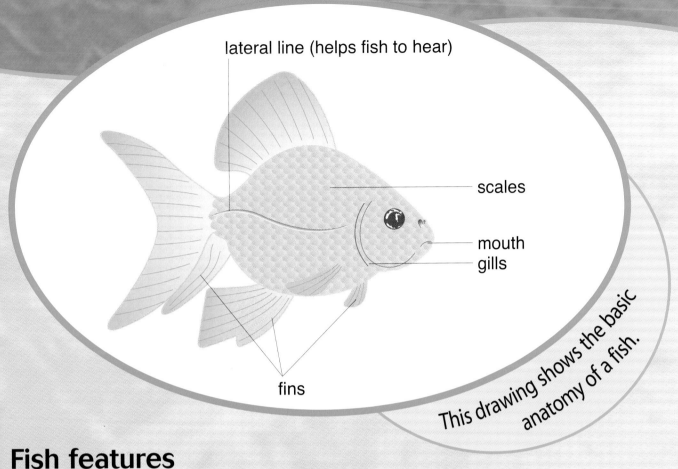

lateral line (helps fish to hear)

scales

mouth

gills

fins

This drawing shows the basic anatomy of a fish.

Fish features

Your pet fish will also have scales, fins and gills.
It may also have large eyes or extra-long fins.

Normally fish have seven fins. The veil tail goldfish
has really large, veil-like fins. Large fins can be
damaged very easily if they are nibbled by other
fish or get caught on things.

Some fish are kept specially for their looks.
For instance, koi carp have many different colours
and patterns.

13

How do fish breathe?

Fish get **oxygen** from the water that they swim in. The **gills** take in oxygen, and the oxygen goes into the fish's blood. Most fish have four pairs of gills and sharks can have seven.

You can sometimes see labyrinth fish gulping air from the water's surface.

Breathing air

Labyrinth fish can also breathe air. They live in lakes in Africa and Asia that do not have very much oxygen in the water because they are drying up. So the fish have developed a special way of breathing air.

Oxygen

Your fish must have plenty of oxygen in its water. You can use a pump that runs bubbles through the water all the time. The movement of the bubbles puts oxygen into the water.

It is important not to take fish out of water because they cannot breathe.

If you see your fish gasping at the top of the **aquarium**, there may not be enough oxygen in the water. Make sure the pump is working and the water is moving in the tank.

Gills, like these, take in oxygen from the water.

15

Senses

Most fish are colour-blind. They cannot see colours like people do. But fish can see shade, reflections, shape and movement.

Pressure warning
*Many fish can feel any change in the water **pressure** around them caused by movement. This warns them if **predators** are near.*

Fish do not have ears. They feel sound through **vibrations** in the water.

Fish have taste buds in and around their mouths. They can taste their food well.

Some fish, like catfish, have taste buds on whiskers around their mouths.

Pet fish have the same senses as wild fish. They use their eyes to find their way around. They use their taste buds when they eat so it is important to give them food they will like.

Protection

Keep fish out of direct sunlight because they cannot close their eyes to protect them.

Fish do not have eyelids.

Do not keep your fish anywhere noisy because the vibrations can disturb them. A sudden bang on an **aquarium** can kill a fish!

Movement

In the wild, fish hardly ever stay still and often have to swim against **currents** in rivers or oceans. Most of a fish's body is made of muscle.

Fish first use the muscles down one side of their bodies and then the other. This makes the body bend and moves the tail from side to side. This is why fish swim in a wriggling motion.

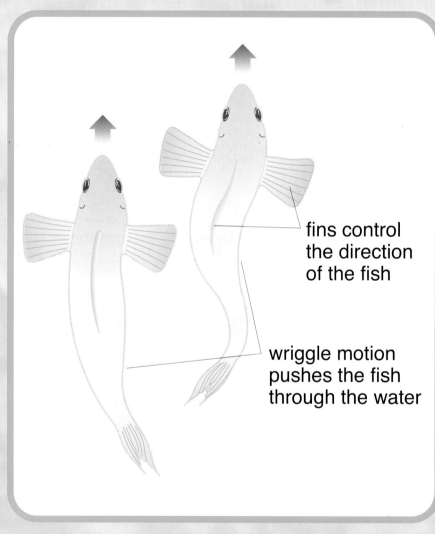

fins control the direction of the fish

wriggle motion pushes the fish through the water

This drawing shows how fish swim.

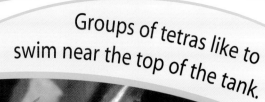

Groups of tetras like to swim near the top of the tank.

Space to swim

Pet fish must have plenty of room to keep swimming. If fish do not have enough room, they may attack each other or injure themselves by swimming into the sides of the tank. Some fish can only take in **oxygen** when they are swimming.

Some fish like to swim in groups, called **schools**. They need lots of space. Other fish like to stay still, just floating in the water.

19

What do fish eat?

Fish can be **carnivores**, which means they eat meat. Other fish are **herbivores** and eat only plants. Some fish are **omnivores** and eat a bit of both.

Food chain

The **food chain** starts with tiny plants and animals called plankton. These are eaten by small fish. Then the small fish are eaten by bigger fish, sharks and other **predators**.

Fish that eat plankton include coldwater fish, like herring. Many fish, such as tuna and sharks, eat other smaller fish.

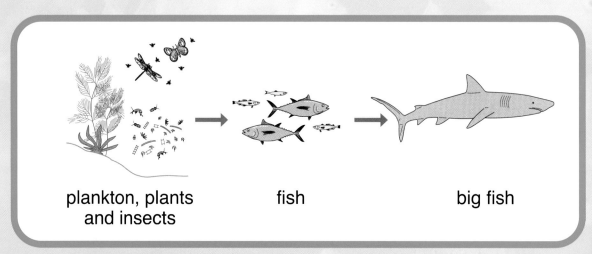

| plankton, plants and insects | fish | big fish |

This is how fish fit into a food chain.

There are many types of fish food.

Just like fish in the wild, pet fish can be carnivores, herbivores or omnivores.

You can buy them live food such as worms, brine shrimps or even

Food colouring
Goldfish need to have special food, which you can buy from your pet shop. If they do not get the right food they lose their gold colour.

small tadpoles. You can also get dried food, like flakes, powders, tablets or freeze-dried worms.

Check with your vet how much food your fish needs. Pet fish can die if you feed them too much.

Do fish live in groups?

Sardines live in schools.

Many fish live in **schools**. This is a large family or group. Living in schools helps to protect fish from **predators**. Some fish, like angelfish and clownfish, live in pairs rather than groups.

Other fish like cod, sharks and barramundi usually live alone. They only ever come together to **mate**.

When you keep fish in an **aquarium**, you need to make sure that you have fish that will live happily together. Some fish will eat or attack other fish. Never put male Siamese fighting fish together. They will fight to the death over their **territory**.

Some fish, like tetras, are school fish. They are best to keep in groups of six or more.

Swordtails like to live in groups. They must have plenty of hiding places as the males can attack the females.

Sleeping

Most fish sleep, but not in the same way as humans. They just blank their minds, a bit like daydreaming.

Some fish that live in the deep ocean, such as sharks and tuna, cannot stop swimming to sleep. They have to keep moving to take in **oxygen**.

Somewhere to sleep

When they are resting, fish like groupers wedge themselves into gravel, a plant or a crack in the rock. Other fish just float in the water.

Parrotfish sleep inside **cocoons** they make every night. The cocoons keep the parrotfish safe from **predators**.

Some fish sleep at night and are awake during the day. These are the best types to have as pets. They will be active when you can look at them. Some fish, like some catfish, are only active at night.

Playing dead

Clown loaches sometimes sleep on their sides at the bottom of the tank. This does not mean that there is anything wrong. You should worry if any fish are rolling about unsteadily as they are probably ill. A fish floating upside down is probably dead.

Life cycle of a fish

Some saltwater fish, such as small reef fish, only live for a few weeks or months. Freshwater fish, like some gobies, live for a year. Sturgeons can live to over 50 years and groupers may live for 80 years.

Breeding

Fish **breed** in several different ways. Some sharks give birth to live young. Other fish, such as sunfish, lay eggs. Sunfish can lay up to 50,000 eggs in one go!

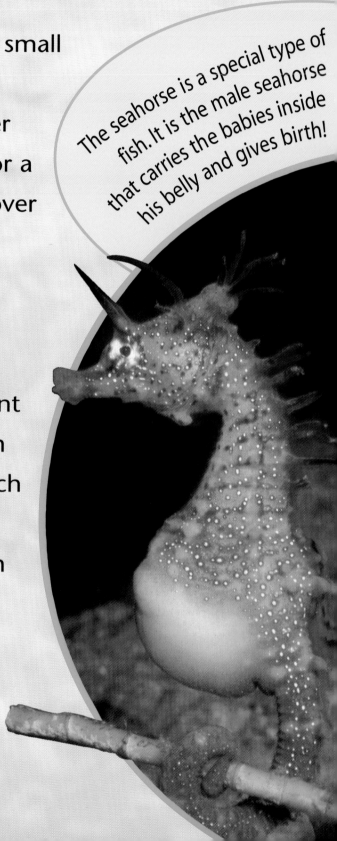

The seahorse is a special type of fish. It is the male seahorse that carries the babies inside his belly and gives birth!

Pet fish can live for a long time. Goldfish can live for 20 years or longer if looked after properly.

Cichlids look after their young. They protect them from danger by keeping them in their mouths.

Fish like cichlids are quite easy to breed in **aquariums**. A pair of convict cichlids will stay together. They make a nest in the gravel to breed. The female lays her eggs and both fish then guard them. After about three to four days, the babies, called fry, hatch out.

Mollies

Mollies are another type of fish that is easy to breed. They give birth to live babies.

Common problems

Fish in the wild are in danger from **pollution** and damage to their **habitats**.

Sometimes people are not responsible about fishing and the waters are over-fished. This means that too many fish are caught. There are fewer and fewer cod in the North Sea because they are being fished before they are adults. Young fish cannot **breed**, so there are no new cod to replace them.

Endangered!

The following fish are endangered:

- *Siberian sturgeon*
- *Alabama sturgeon*
- *Chinese paddlefish*
- *Alabama shad*
- *silver or Bala shark*
- *wild common carp*
- *clanwilliam redfin.*

One danger for wild fish is getting caught for food.

28

These are some common fish problems.

tail or fin rot

cloudy eye

damaged fins

fungus

Buying a pet fish

Always make sure you buy your fish from a good pet shop. Make sure they are not **endangered** fish that have been taken from the wild.

Some fish can have problems if their fins or eyes stick out. Always look out for any damage to fins, eyes or scales. Move any fish that attack other fish or nibble their fins to a different tank.

Find out for yourself

A good owner will always want to learn more about keeping pet fish. To find out more information about fish, you can look in other books and on the Internet.

Books to read

Encylopedia of Tropical Fish, Dick Mills (Interpet Publishing, 1999)

Pets: Goldfish, Michaela Miller (Heinemann Library, 1997)

Using the Internet

Explore the Internet to find out about fish. Websites can change, so if one of the links below no longer works, don't worry. Use a search engine, such as *www.yahooligans.com* or *www.internet4kids.com*. You could try searching with the keywords 'fish', 'pet' and 'wild fish'.

Websites

This website tells you how to set up and look after an aquarium: *www.fishedz.com*

The Goldfish Paradise Society has lots of information about goldfish: *www.goldfishparadise.com*

Disclaimer
All the Internet addresses (URLs) given in this book were valid at the time of going to press. However, due to the dynamic nature of the Internet, some addresses may have changed, or sites may have ceased to exist since publication. While the author and publishers regret any inconvenience this may cause readers, no responsibility for any such changes can be accepted by either the author or the publishers.

Glossary

algae very simple plants

anatomy how the body is made

aquarium special tank for keeping fish in

breed animals mate and have babies

camouflage colour or pattern that lets an animal blend into the background

carnivore animal that only eats meat

cocoon a case woven by an animal, insect or fish

coral reef coral is the skeletons of millions of tiny animals. They can grow over large areas to make reefs.

current flow of air or water

electricity a type of energy

endangered in danger of dying out or being killed

equator imaginary line around the middle of the Earth

food chain the links between different animals that feed on each other and on plants

gills things which fish use to take in oxygen

habitat where an animal or plant lives

herbivore animal that eats only plants

mate two animals come together to make babies

omnivore animal that eats meat, plants and insects

oxygen a gas all living things need to survive

pollution making the environment dirty with waste or poisonous chemicals

predator animal that hunts and eats other animals

pressure the force of water or air on the body or any object

prey animal that is hunted and eaten by other animals

school a big group of fish swimming together

territory the area an animal lives and hunts in

tropical warm parts of the world near the equator

vibration shaking movement

Index

anatomy 12–13
angelfish 5, 6, 8, 20, 22
aquariums 5, 7, 9, 11, 15, 19, 23, 27

breathing 14–15
breeding 26, 27, 28
buying a pet fish 29

camouflage 10
carnivores 20, 21
catfish 16, 25
cichlids 6, 27
coldwater fish 6, 7, 20
coral reefs 10

eels 12
endangered fish 28, 29
eyes and vision 16, 17, 29

fins 8, 12, 13, 29
fish in the wild 4, 6, 7, 8, 10, 16, 18, 20, 22, 24, 26, 28
food 20–21

food chain 20
freshwater fish 8, 9, 26

gills 12, 13, 14, 15
gobies 4, 26
goldfish 7, 13, 21, 27
groups, living in 22–23

habitats 6, 7, 10–11
health 25, 29
herbivores 20, 21

koi carp 5, 13

labyrinth fish 14
life cycle 26–27
lifespan 26, 27
loaches 7, 25

mollies 27

omnivores 20, 21
over-fishing 28
oxygen 14, 15, 19, 24

parrotfish 24
pet fish 5, 7, 9, 11, 13, 15, 17, 19, 21, 23, 25, 27, 29
piranhas 6, 10

plankton 20
predators 10, 12, 16, 20, 22, 24

rays 10
reef fish 10, 26

saltwater fish 8, 9, 26
scales 12, 13, 29
schools 19, 22, 23
seahorses 26
senses 16–17
sharks 4, 20, 22, 24, 26, 28
Siamese fighting fish 23
sleeping 24–25
swimming 18–19
swordtails 23

taste buds 16, 17
tetras 9, 19, 23
tropical fish 6, 7

vibrations 16, 17

water-plants 10, 11

young fish 22, 26, 27

Titles in the *Wild Side of Pets* series include:

Hardback   1 844 43479 6

Hardback   1 844 43478 8

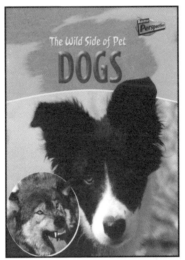

Hardback   1 844 43480 X

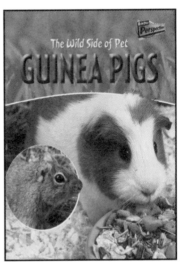

Hardback   1 844 43483 4

Hardback   1 844 43481 8

Hardback   1 844 43482 6

Find out about the other titles in this series on our website www.raintreepublishers.co.uk